Working Towards
DESIRABLE OUTCOMES

A PHOTOCOPIABLE ACTIVITY BOOK

Mary Wright

Towards The Desirable Learning Outcomes For Young Children

A 12 Week Programme

focusing on:

- Mathematics

- Language and Literacy

- Knowledge and Understand of the World

Designed for small groups working with adult support.

The suggested activities are only part of the Early Years Curriculum, other areas being covered by the ongoing work of the setting.

Working Towards Desirable Outcomes

A Photocopiable Activity Book

by Mary Wright

Introduction

Working Towards Desirable Outcomes is a 64 page teacher resource book containing ideas and photocopiable worksheets for use with Nursery/Reception children. The book is split into twelve sections which may be taught over a twelve week period to prepare for entry to compulsory education.

Practical small group activities are used to encourage making and doing within an active pre-school environment. The pages are simply laid out to enable the busy teacher to select appropriate ideas, choose from the photocopiable sheets and develop or extend them as appropriate to their own situation.

Activities are suggested for Mathematics, Language & Literacy and Knowledge and Understanding of the World - the three main areas outlined in the "Desirable Outcomes for Children's Learning Document".

Copyright © 1998 Mary Wright
Illustrated by Paul Sealey
Printed in Great Britain for "Topical Resources", Publishers of Educational Materials, P.O. Box 329, Preston PR3 5LT

(Tel/Fax 01772 863158)

by T.Snape & Company Ltd, Boltons Court, Preston.
Layout & Cover Design by Paul Sealey Illustration & Design, 3 Wentworth Drive, Thornton. 01253 865575

First Published January 1998
ISBN 1 872977 30 8

Contents

Overview P.4

WEEK 1
Suggested Activities P.5
Instructions for photocopiable pages P.6
Mathematics P.7
Language and Literacy P.8
Knowledge and Understanding of the World P.9

WEEK 2
Suggested Activities P.10
Instructions for photocopiable pages P.11
Mathematics P.12
Language and Literacy P.13
Knowledge and Understanding of the World P.14

WEEK 3
Suggested Activities P.15
Instructions for photocopiable pages P.16
Mathematics P.17
Language and Literacy P.18
Knowledge and Understanding of the World. P.19

WEEK 4
Suggested Activities P.20
Instructions for photocopiable pages P.21
Mathematics P.22
Language and Literacy P.23
Knowledge and Understanding of the World P.24

WEEK 5
Suggested Activities P.25
Instructions for photocopiable pages P.26
Mathematics P.27
Language and Literacy P.28
Knowledge and Understanding of the World P.29

WEEK 6
Suggested Activities P.30
Instructions for photocopiable pages P.31
Mathematics P.32
Language and Literacy P.33
Knowledge and Understanding of the World P.34

WEEK 7
Suggested Activities P.35
Instructions for photocopiable pages P.36
Mathematics P.37
Language and Literacy P.38
Knowledge and Understanding of the World P.39

WEEK 8
Suggested Activities P.40
Instructions for photocopiable pages P.41
Mathematics P.42
Language and Literacy P.43
Knowledge and Understanding of the World P.44

WEEK 9
Suggested Activities P.45
Instructions for photocopiable pages P.46
Mathematics P.47
Language and Literacy P.48
Knowledge and Understanding of the World P.49

WEEK 10
Suggested Activities P.50
Instructions for photocopiable pages P.51
Mathematics P.52
Language and Literacy P.53
Knowledge and Understanding of the World P.54

WEEK 11
Suggested Activities P.55
Instructions for photocopiable pages P.56
Mathematics P.57
Language and Literacy P.58
Knowledge and Understanding of the World P.59

WEEK 12
Suggested Activities P.60
Instructions for photocopiable pages P.61
Mathematics P.62
Language and Literacy P.63
Knowledge and Understanding of the World P.64

Overview

- **M** Mathematics
- **LL** Language and Literacy
- **KUW** Knowledge and Understanding of the World

Week 1	Week 2	Week 3
M Number 1 / Shape	**M** Size / Weighing	**M** Number 2
LL Aa Bb	**LL** Cc Dd	**LL** Ee Ff
KUW Colour / Weather / The Park	**KUW** Cooking / Food From Other Countries	**KUW** Our Senses - Hearing - Outdoor Sounds
Week 4	**Week 5**	**Week 6**
M Dice Patterns / Games	**M** Number 3	**M** Number 4 / Height
LL Gg Hh	**LL** Ii Jj	**LL** Kk Ll
KUW Our Senses - Touch **Clothes Around the World**	**KUW** Our Senses - Sight **Going to School**	**KUW** Our Senses - Smell - Taste
Week 7	**Week 8**	**Week 9**
M Number 5	**M** Number 6	**M** Number 7
LL Mm Nn	**LL** Oo Pp	**LL** Qq Uu Rr
KUW Melting / Cold Countries	**KUW** Floating and Sinking / Boats	**KUW** Magnets
Week 10	**Week 11**	**Week 12**
M Number 8 / Positions	**M** Number 9 / Time	**M** Number 10 / Money
LL Ss Tt	**LL** Vv Ww	**LL** Xx Yy Zz
KUW Soap / Water / Washing	**KUW** Growing Seeds	**KUW** Camouflage

Suggested Activities - Week 1

Mathematics - Recognising and Understanding the Number 1 / Shape.

Number 1 snake game

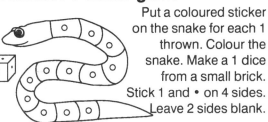

Put a coloured sticker on the snake for each 1 thrown. Colour the snake. Make a 1 dice from a small brick. Stick 1 and • on 4 sides. Leave 2 sides blank.

Make a zig-zag shape book.

Stick different sizes for each shape.

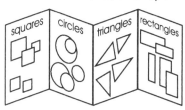

Match the shape part.

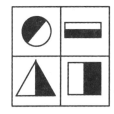

Give each cat a tail.

Stick a cat in each space. Draw tail and write number 1

Language and Literacy - Letter Aa Letter Bb

Aa Animal guessing game.

Talk about different animals.
Can you guess which animal I am thinking about :-
I have stripes and I live in a jungle (tiger).
I am very big and have a trunk (elephant).

When I am awake
I move about
I eat and drink
I talk and laugh

When I am asleep
I lie still
I breathe
I snore

Aeroplanes at the airport

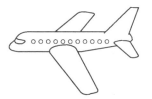

Cut out some aeroplane shapes. Draw an airport to stick them on - runway, tower etc.

Bb Play games with bat, balls, bean bags, and balloons.

Can you balance a bean bag on your back?

Stick some black, blue, brown shapes or beads, material scraps onto a b shape.

Make a blue paper beanbag.

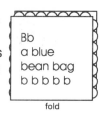

Fold paper in half. Draw little beans inside, or use card and stick real beans firmly inside. Staple up the sides. Peep through top to see beans. Practice writing Bb, colour blue, or use blue paper.

Knowledge and Understanding of the World - Colour, Weather, The Park.

Colours -talk about favourite colours and what we chose to wear. Some colours make us feel happy, like yellow, others are cool colours like blue.

Rainbows - When do we see them? How are they made? - (by raindrops splitting sunlight into all its colours.)

Story - The Rainbow Balloon -
*Fredun Shapur -
Simon & Schuster Young Books*

Look - through a Kaleidoscope.

Make - a weather picture.

Going to the park

What do we see on the way? - houses, shops, gardens, etc.
Where is the park? - a long journey or a short journey?
Would you walk, catch a bus, go by car?
What sort of weather is best in the park? - rainy for splashing in puddles, windy for flying kites, sunny for eating ice-cream?

People in the park - whom might you see there? - mums, dads, children, old people sitting or walking?

Animals in the park - squirrels, birds, ducks, dogs, hedgehogs.

Instructions for Photocopiable Activities - Week 1

Mathematics
Make a shape dragon

Cut out the dragon for the children and use the shape templates to cut out the shapes in bright colours. The children can practice pencil skills drawing round the shapes on the dragon, and then stick on the matching coloured shapes.

Talk about the names of the shapes, colours, the number of sides and corners, and where they might see those shapes every day e.g. - bricks, cereal boxes, windows, bicycle wheels, cheese wedges. Encourage early reading skills by pointing to the words - 'my shape dragon'.

Language and Literacy
Make an apron for apples

The children cut around the apron and fold up the bottom. Staple this at the sides and in the middle to make 2 pockets. They can help to sellotape wool ties at the sides and round the top.

Cut out several apples for the children to practice writing Aa on, to be put in the pockets.

The apron can be decorated by the children - for example with handwriting patterns going from left to right. They can stick 1 red apple and 1 green apple on the front of the pockets. Point out the letter 'a' in apron and apple.

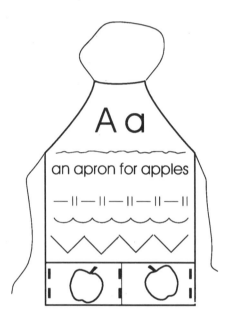

Knowledge and Understanding of the World
Make a rainbow balloon

The children cut around the balloon and attach some wool or string to it with sellotape on the back.

Talk about the colours in the rainbow and how they come in a certain order - red, orange, yellow, green, blue, indigo (pink) violet (purple).

Help them notice that black, brown and white are not in the rainbow. Some children may be able to colour, felt tip or paint with small brushes, the colours in the right order. Other children may just enjoy using colours as they choose.

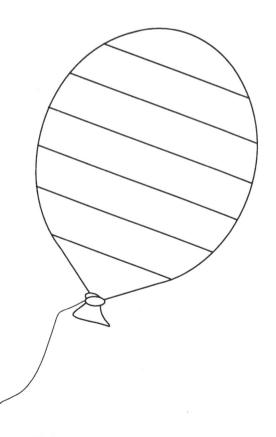

Language and Literacy - Week 1

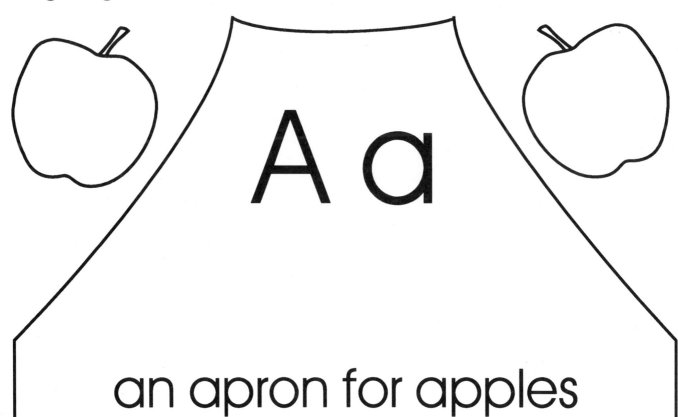

A a

an apron for apples

Knowledge and Understanding of the World - Week 1

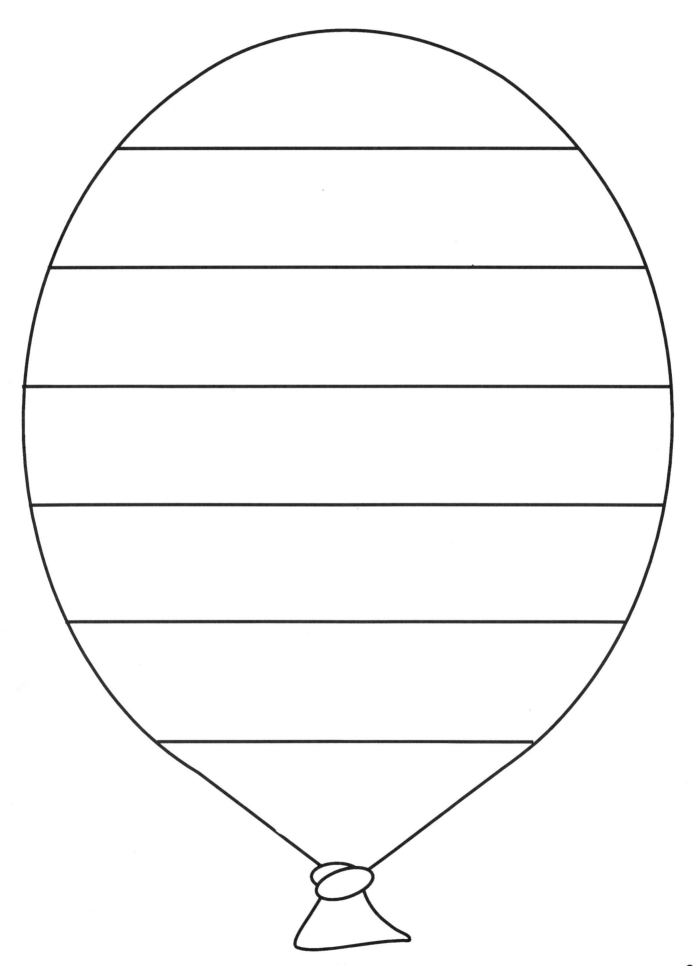

Suggested Activities - Week 2

Mathematics - Using Mathematical Language - Size / Weighing / Heavy & Light

What's missing game

Spread out the big and small shapes, talking about each one. Let the children close their eyes, cover the shapes and remove one. Which one is missing? eg. the big circle.

Heavy and Light

Weigh
eg. conkers, corks, pine cones, stones, small bricks, lids, leaves etc.
Talk about heavy and light things.
Let the children feel objects and predict what will happen on the scale.
Talk about why we weigh things and talk about different types of scale - bathroom, kitchen, post office, supermarket, etc. Talk about balance.

Story - Can't You Sleep Little Bear?
Martin Waddell & Barbara Firth - Walker Books.

Divide up some paper so that the children can draw big bear and little bear at each end. Let them make patterns on paper for a big and little duvet.

Language and Literacy - Letter Cc Letter Dd

Cc What makes me feel:-

 - when things aren't fair, when someone touches my things etc.

 - Things I can do - cook, cut, colour with crayons, copy, curl, clap, count.

Can you count the carrots?

Put them in order - largest, smallest. Cut out carrots from orange paper or roll orange playdough.

Dd Do some dancing to a drum

Listening skills - Which is the odd word out?

• Duck, door, pig, dad.
• Dog, don't, dot, me.

Join dot-to-dot pictures - eg: dog.

Put some ducks in the duck pond

Make a blue pond with bits of green tissue weed. Colour or paint ducks to stick on. Put a "d" on each duck.

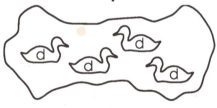

Knowledge and Understanding of the World - Cooking / Foods and Where They Come From

Cake
Make a cake - a big cake or little cup cakes. Introduce words like "ingredients" and "recipe". Talk about the changes that take place during cooking.
- dry ingredients - flour, sugar, cocoa.
- wet ingredients - eggs, milk, margarine.
What happens to the mixture in the oven?

Talk about different cooking techniques, mixing, sieving, grating, beating, whisking.

Use kitchen scales to measure ingredients.

Safety - Hot ovens, taking care, washing hands.

Favourite foods
Where do they come from? Are they grown here or in other countries?
Look at labels to see where they are made or grown. Make an exotic fruit basket.

Look at some old objects in the kitchen from the past - scales, kettles, wash boards, storage jars etc.

Instructions for Photocopiable Activities - Week 2

Mathematics
Big and Little

Talk about size and ask the children which things they think are big, little, large, small. Show how size is comparative - e.g. Mummy is big but smaller than a tree. Let the children draw pictures of big things on the elephant, such as a lorry, bus, house, car, tree, and stick little things on the mouse - a button, a pen, a little shell, a paper clip, a small bead etc. Alternatively the children could cut out appropriate magazine pictures. Look at the words to help children recognise big and little.

Language and Literacy
Cut Some Colourful Candles

Cut out the photocopied shape for the children. Fold up the bottom part and staple to make a pocket. Fold the C over and help the children practice writing C on it. The children can colour the candles and cut them out to fit in the pocket. Talk about cutting, colouring and candles all beginning with C, and let the children point out the C's on the writing - "cut some colourful candles."

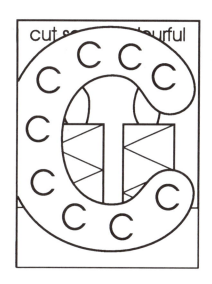

Knowledge and Understanding of the World

Make a cake with the children talking about the different ingredients and how to make it. Look at several recipe books and cards, talking about the different information they contain and how helpful it is to have some instructions. Let the children cut round the recipe card and cut in between the little pictures. Point out the words for the ingredients and help them to match and stick the pictures onto the card. Perhaps they could remember the process of how to make the cake. What did they do first etc.?

11

Mathematics - Week 2

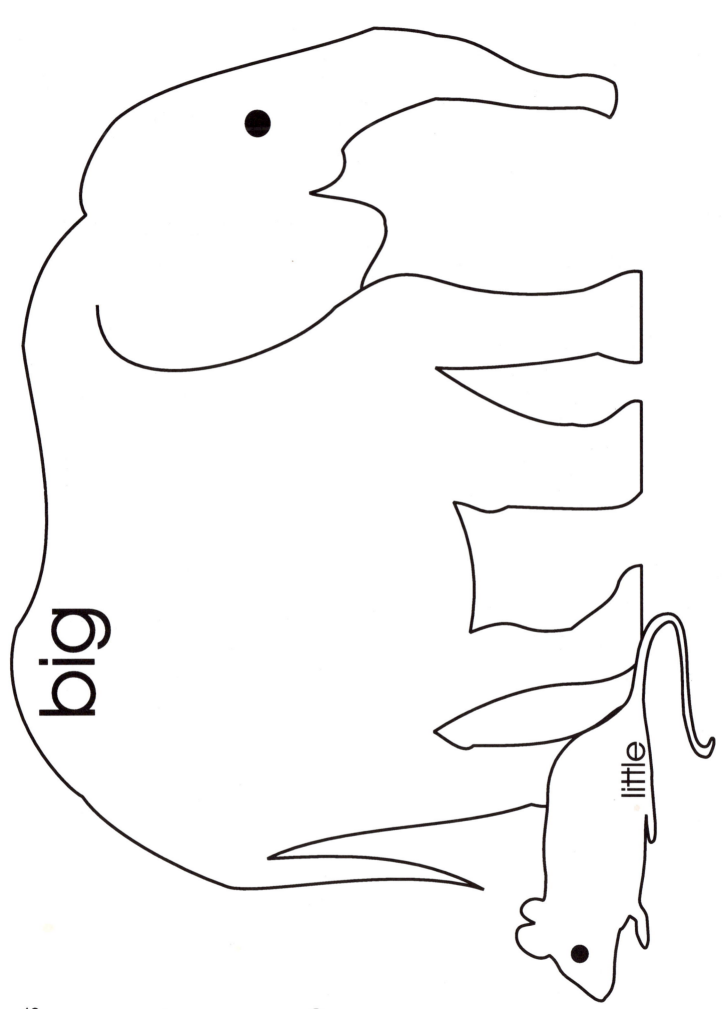

Language and Literacy - Week 2

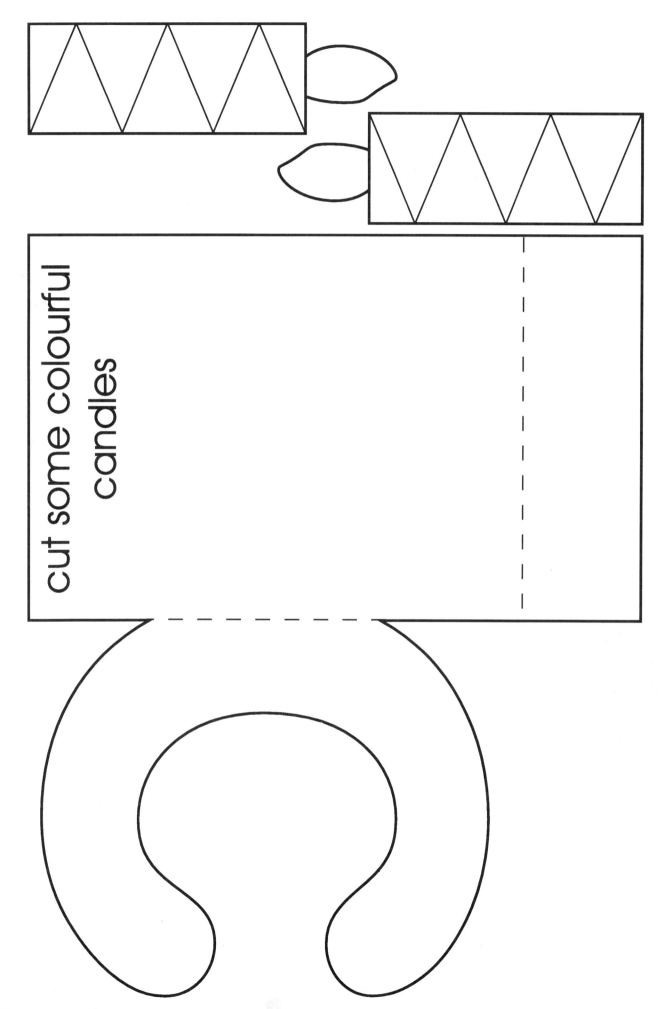

cut some colourful candles

Knowledge and Understanding of the World - Week 2

Suggested Activities - Week 3

Mathematics - Recognising and Understanding Number 2

Matching 2 game

Collect 2 sets of the same small toys. Put one set in a bag and spread out the other. Children choose from the bag and find the matching toy. They place them on a giant 2 shape.

Patterns
Paint a picture with 2 colours. Use 2 colours of peg and pegboard to make a pattern. Thread 2 colours of wooden beads on a lace to make a pattern.

Things I can do
 - with hands and feet.

 - I can see with 2 eyes

- I can hear with 2 ears

Match pairs of socks
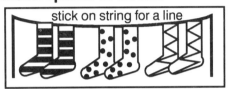
Let the children cut out sock shapes with patterns on. They can colour, match and stick them on the line.

Find 2 pictures the same
Play snap, or memory game - put some cards face down. Turn 2 over at a time. Replace if not a pair. Children take turns until they find pairs.

Number 2 wheel
Children can stick 2 things the same in each segment. Use pasta, buttons, shapes, material scraps, etc.

Language and Literacy - Letter Ee Letter Ff

Ee Make an envelope of eggs
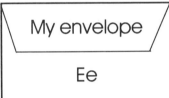

Let the children cut round the egg shapes, draw and colour a pattern on one side, and practice **e** on the other. Put the eggs in an envelope.

Energetic exercises
Talk about using our energy, and food that gives us energy. Do some exercises together.

Play a game
I *enjoy* clapping .

I *enjoy* clapping and _____

Talk about *electric* things in the house - kettle, iron, lights, washing machine, cooker etc.

Ff Follow some footprints

Stick some shapes on some cut out feet - triangle, circle, moon, star etc. The children name the shapes as they step on them.
Let the children do **finger painting on a Friday.**

Play a fishing game
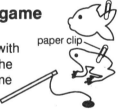
-for frogs or fish. Make a fishing rod with a magnet end. Let the children cut out some fish or frogs

Knowledge and Understanding of the World - Our Senses / Hearing

Hearing
Let the children create sounds using a variety of junk materials e.g. paper bags, tubes, newspaper, crackly paper, old keys, shakers, tins with an object in, spoons - wooden and metal - by tapping, shaking, scraping, flicking, scrunching, rubbing and tearing.

Find 2 sounds the same
Make pairs of old film tubes with matching sounds by filling them with peas, sand, buttons etc. Children shake them to find out the tubes with matching sounds.
Talk about sounds I hear outside.
Talk about nice sounds and scary sounds - laughter, screaming etc.

Sounds in the town
Cars, lorries reversing, horns, buses, heavy trucks, road works, sirens, birds, aeroplanes, alarms, church bells, people chattering, etc.

Sounds that might be different in the country
Cows, tractors, waterfalls, horses hooves, trains, sheep, etc.

Song - Sounds I Hear (Tinderbox)

Instructions for Photocopiable Activities - Week 3

Mathematics
Number 2 - Match identical twins
Cut out the grid for the children. Let them cut along between the faces, and stick side by side 2 faces that are the same.

The children practice writing number 2.

Language and Literacy
Flip a funny face
Copy 2 sheets. Cut out the 2 faces for the children. Let them cut around the shirts if they can.

The children draw 2 funny faces and stick them back to back on a long strip of card or dowel.

On one shirt they practice writing Ff. Colour patterns on the other.

The children glue only the edges of the shirts and stick together with the card strip in between so that it will flip (turn) round between the shirts.

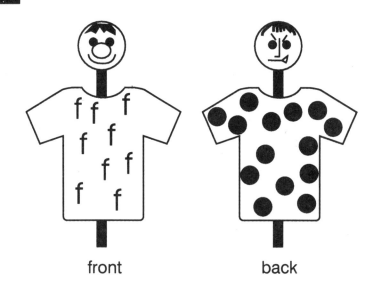

front   back

Knowledge and Understanding of the World
Follow a pattern of sounds

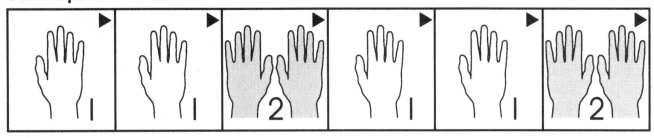

Place the hand pattern strips in front of the children so they can tap on a table or their knees. Help them to follow the strips from left to right, putting one hand or two hands together on the table according to the picture, to build up a pattern of sound.

The strips can be extended by photocopying twice, and joining together, or cut up for the children to make their own patterns. Try fast / slow, loudly / softly.

Mathematics - Week 3

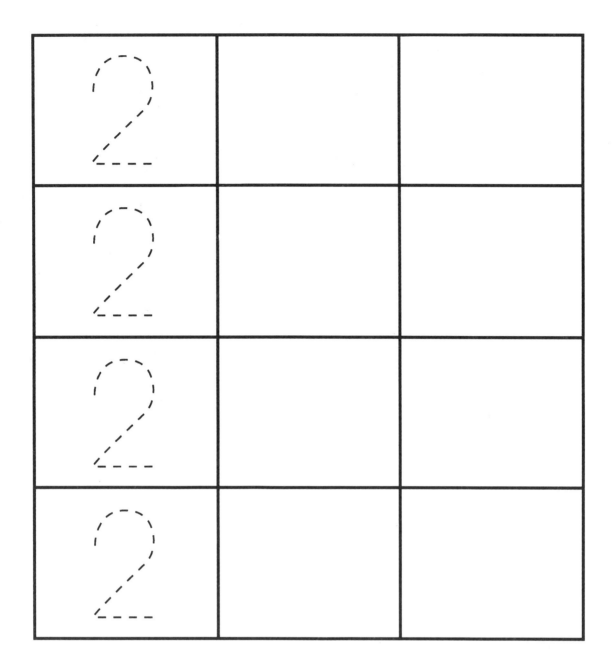

Language and Literacy - Week 3

Knowledge and Understanding of the World - Week 3

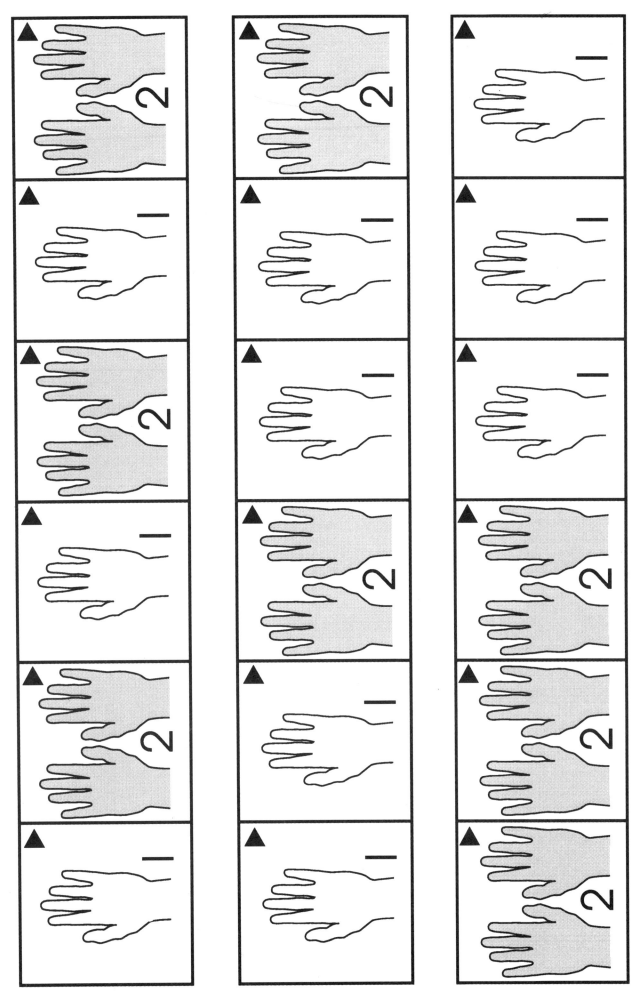

© Topical Resources. May be photocopied for classroom use only.

Suggested Activities - Week 4

Mathematics - Recognising Dice Patterns / Playing Games

Focus on the dice patterns rather than counting dots.

Match the patterns to the numbers.
Colour and cut out the dice squares. Match them and stick under the numbers.

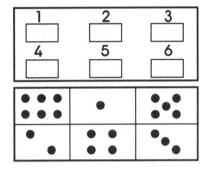

Make a dice
Colour the dice squares. Children need help to fold into a dice.

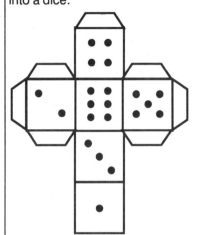

The old woman who lived in a shoe

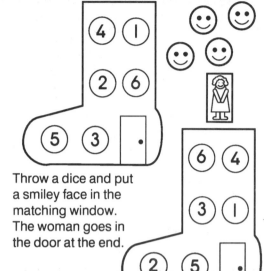

Throw a dice and put a smiley face in the matching window. The woman goes in the door at the end.

Language and Literacy - Letter Gg Letter Hh

Gg Listening carefully and following instructions

 and touch the door
and find 2 pencils
and bring back something red.

 a hug
your favourite doll
a wooden brick.

 what I am thinking of:-
Gate, grapes, girl, gift, goat.

Make a garden
Make tissue flowers and tuck into a brown pocket. Practice **g**.

Hh Hot things

Sun **flames** **cookers** **pans** **drinks**

What makes things hot? How can we tell they are hot - steam, smoke, feeling heat?

Keeping safe near hot things - taking care about touching or knocking things over.

When do we feel hot? - after exercise, near heaters or fires, sunny days, hot baths?

Play hop scotch

Knowledge and Understanding of the World - Our Senses / Touch / Clothes Around the World

Touch
Talk about the different feelings we get when we touch things such as rough, smooth, prickly, furry, hard, soft, hot, cold, silky, slimy, sticky, sharp etc.

Have a 'feely' bag with a selection of things in - eg. a conker, fir cone, pencil, wool, soft toy, hair curler, sellotape, stone, sandpaper, feather, etc.
Ask the children to feel objects before looking.

Costumes and clothes around the world
Talk about the clothes we like to wear and what they are made of - wool, cotton, leather, etc.

Look at and compare different costumes and clothes from other countries - different patterns, fabrics, hats, clothes for keeping warm or cool etc.

Look at pictures of clothes in the past - e.g. Victorian clothes. How are they different from clothes now?

Instructions for Photocopiable Activities - Week 4

Mathematics
A game - Bees in the Beehive
Let the children cut around the bees on the dotted lines, and cut out the hive, ready to play the game. The children shake the dice and put the matching bee into the hive. The winner is the first to have all the bees in the hive. The bees and hive could be coloured either before or at the end of the game. NB. Look at the pattern on the dice rather than counting the dots. Keep the game flowing by telling the children the number until the have confidence with dice patterns. Encourage early ready by pointing to the words bees in the beehive.

Language and Literacy
Make a hanger for some hats
Photocopy the hanger onto card if possible and cut out for the children, including the centre part. Let the children colour and cut round the hats. These can be attached either by taping wool to the backs of the hats and hanger, or by punching holes and tying the wool. The children can practice writing Hh, and recognise the 'h' sound in 'hanger' and 'hats'.

Knowledge and Understanding of the World
Touch - make a feely Humpty Dumpty on a wall
Let the children cut round Humpty and colour in his face. Have a selection of different kinds of fabric bits for the children to stick on the bottom part of Humpty - eg. felt, furry material, towelling, silky lining, cotton wool etc. Encourage them to talk about what the pieces feel like. Cut out some arms and legs for the children in a contrasting material e.g.- shiny plastic, foil.
Let them make their own hat from either paper or fabric. Cut out some rough sandpaper bricks for the children to stick on for a wall. Humpty Dumpty can be stapled or stuck against the top of the wall.

Mathematics - Week 4

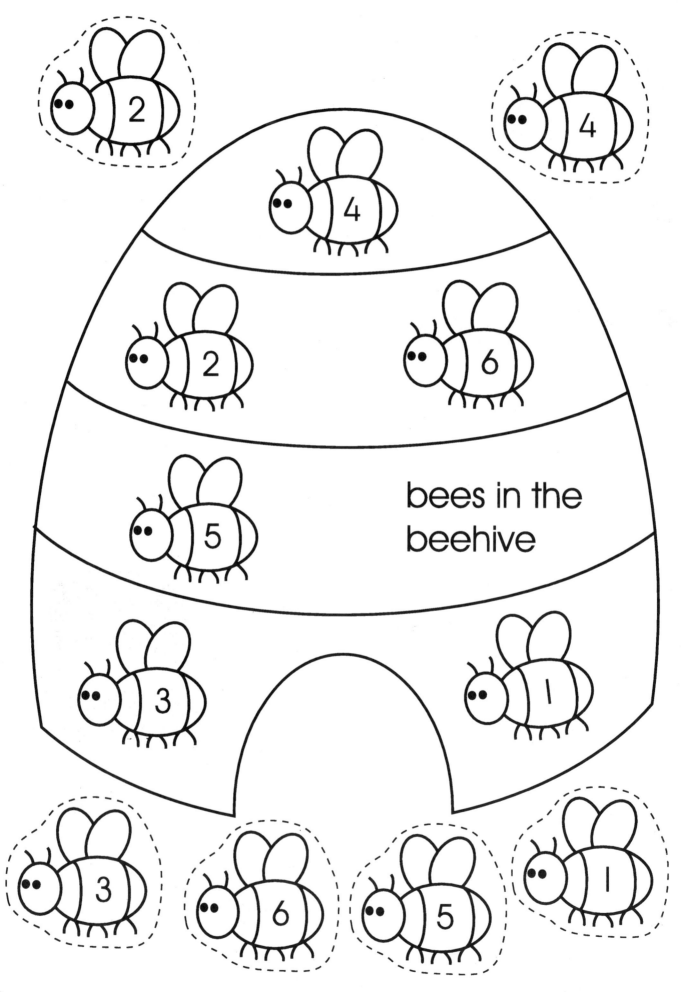

bees in the beehive

Language and Literacy - Week 4

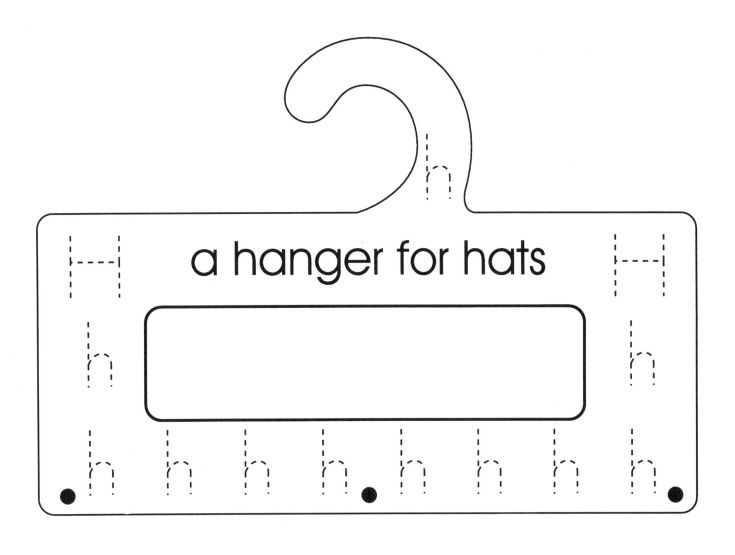

Knowledge and Understanding of the World - Week 4

Suggested Activities - Week 5

Mathematics - Recognising and Understanding Number 3

Paint a 3
Cut out a 3 shape. Paint it in stripes using 3 colours. Mount on card or paper and hang up.

Nursery rhymes
Baa Baa Black Sheep
...... 3 bags full.

Make patterns with 3 colours
- use little pegs and peg boards, links, threading beads, cubes, bricks etc.

Make 3 blind mice
Cut out a mouse shape on folded paper, with the fold at the top. Open up and stick the ears on each piece together so the mouse will stand. Stick the tail end together with wool in between for the tail. Add some wool whiskers and cut up some plasters to stick as patches over the eyes. Make a nest from a cereal box and tissue.

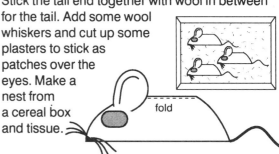

Make a card jigsaw in 3 pieces
Draw lines on an old card. Let the children cut it into 3 pieces and put in a stapled pocket.

my 3 piece puzzle

Language and Literacy - Letter Ii Letter Jj

Ii In - inside
How many boxes can you fit inside each other? (Use a selection of cereal and small boxes).
Play with Russian dolls fitting inside each other.
Talk about things to play with inside rather then outside.

Insects
Where do they live - under stones, logs, tree trunks etc.

When I feel ill
I like a cuddle.
I like to be quiet.
I like someone to take care of me.

Jj Tell some funny jokes

Join things together
Using paper clips, staples, glue, split pins, safety pins, tape, tags, string etc.

Jumping
Practice big jumps, little jumps, fast and slow jumps.

Junk modelling
Make a jeep using old cereal boxes, lids, tops etc.

Juice
My favourite flavour of *juice* is _____.
Try different varieties.

Knowledge and Understanding of the World - Our Senses / Sight / Going to School

Sight
Play - 'Guess who it is'. Feel someone when blindfolded - use touch and hearing to identify them.

Talk about eye tests and visiting the optician. Why do people where glasses, contact lenses, sun glasses etc?

Talk about colours we see during daylight in contrast to grey at night.

Make some glasses with cellophane lenses.
Cut out the eye part and stick coloured cellophane on the inside.

Talk about blind people and how they find their way about, using a white stick, or a guide dog.

How can we help? - by not leaving things around to trip over.

What did you see coming to school today? e.g.- busy roads, car park, supermarket, traffic lights, church, fields, special local features, new buildings, old buildings etc.

Instructions for Photocopiable Activities - Week 5

Mathematics
The 3 bears game
Make a number 3 dice using a small cubed brick. Cut out the photocopiable dice squares and stick on four sides of the cube, leaving two sides blank. To play the game throw the dice and put a counter or sticky spot on one of the bears' buttons for every 3 thrown. The winner has all the bears' buttons covered. Talk about the size of the bears and point out the words - daddy, mummy, baby. The bears can be coloured at the end of the game. Count how many buttons altogether.

Language and Literacy
A jar of jam
Talk about jars of jam, different flavours and fruits used. Let the children taste some or make jam sandwiches. Read the story "The Giant Jam Sandwich" *Lord John Vernon - Piper Books.*
The children can cut round the jam jar and fold it over. They can colour the front red and practice writing j on the back. Inside, the children could either cut and stick some more strawberries from red paper, or draw some different fruits used for jam.

Knowledge and Understanding of the World
Eyes
Let the children look at their own eyes in a mirror. Talk about their eye colour and some of the parts of the eye e.g.- pupil, eyelashes, eyelids, eyebrows. Colour in the eyes on the photocopiable sheet and complete their own face. Point to the words and let them fill in their own eye colour.

Mathematics - Week 5

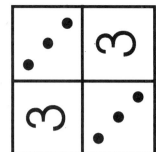

Language and Literacy - Week 5

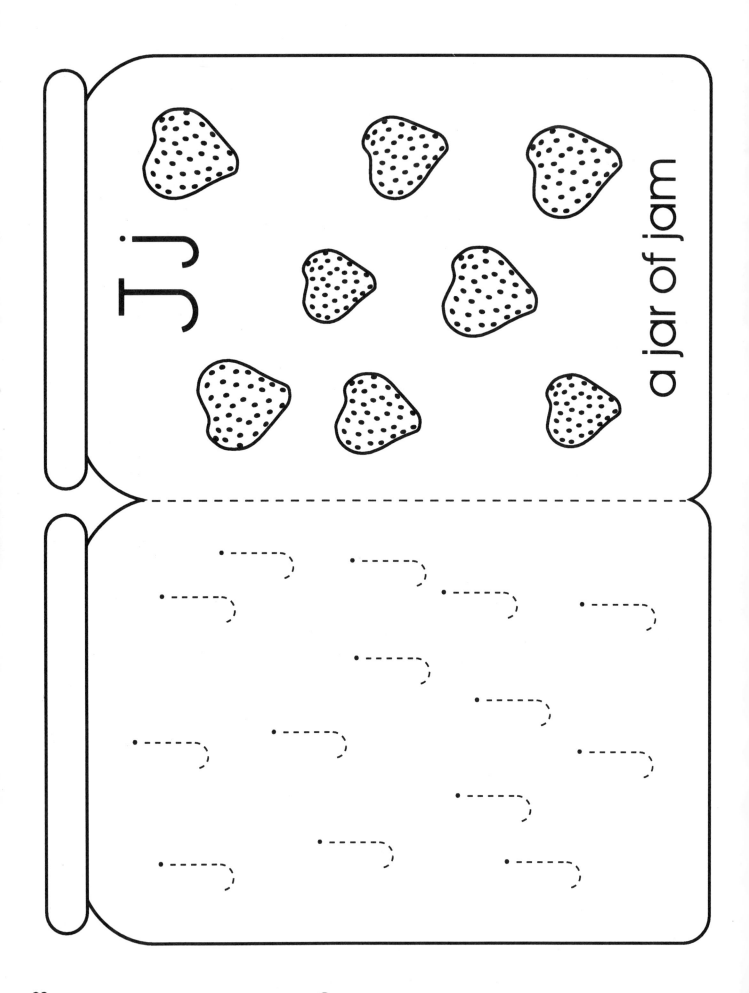

a jar of jam

Knowledge and Understanding of the World - Week 5

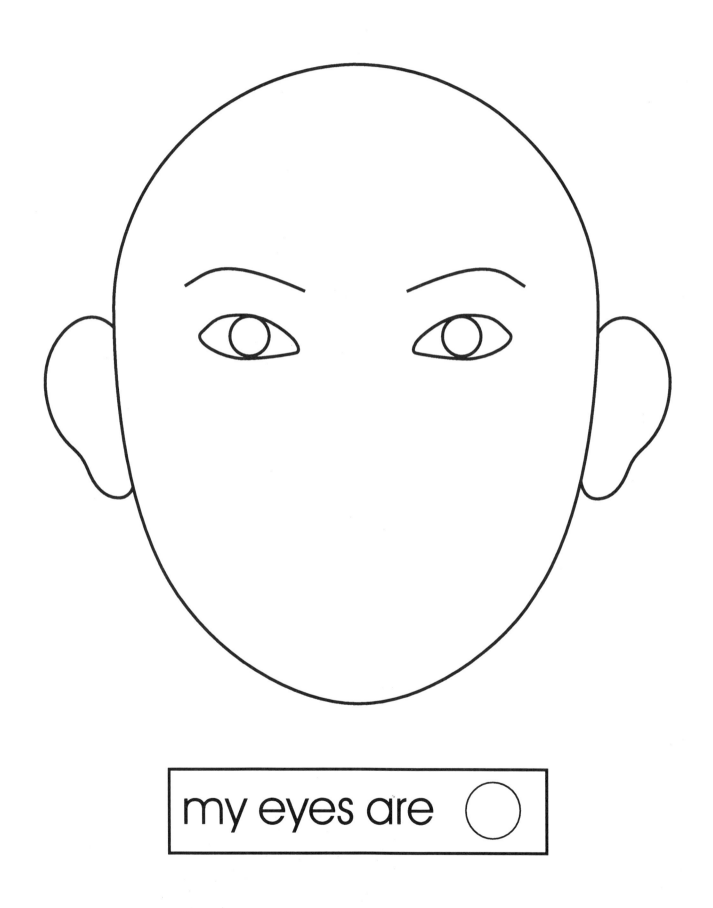

Suggested Activities - Week 6

Mathematics - Recognising and Understanding Number 4 / Height

Folding into 4
Fold a square into 4. Stick 4 small playdough shapes in each quarter.

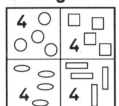

What makes 4
Discuss, using 2 colours. Print spots with a cork using 2 colours.

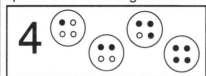

Who is the tallest 4 year old?
Record height on a strip of paper folded up and tucked into a pocket.

Number 4 game
Use a cube to make a 4 dice. Stick 4 onto 4 sides leave 2 sides blank. Stick on 4 coloured sticky spots in a truck for each 4 thrown.

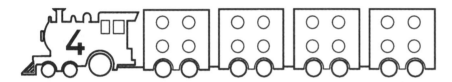

Tall and short buildings
Snip strips of yellow for windows.

Language and Literacy - Letter Kk Letter Ll

Kk Make a beautiful kite
Paint, or stick on collage bits

Kind people - what do they do?

Keys
Sort into size and shape. Imagine to whom they belong and where they might fit e.g.- a giant in a castle.

Things we do in the kitchen
Cook our meals, wash up the saucepans, dry the dishes, do the washing etc.

What is kept in the kitchen?
Food, cups, plates.

Ll Make Mr. Longlegs
Practice Ll on the hat. Make long Concertina strips for legs.

Long ladders short ladders
Which would the window cleaner use for a tall building?

Write long lists.

My list
lips
lettuce
light
library
lamb
leaf
lemon

Knowledge and Understanding of the World - Our Senses - Smell / Taste

Smell
Have a selection of little pots to smell - e.g. curry powder, a tub rinsed with TCP, lavender, perfume, aftershave, smelly cheese etc. Include nice and nasty smells.
Talk about smells outside - flowers, smoke, after the rain, fumes, chips etc.

Draw a picture of me
Have a pocket with a tissue or a piece of material sprinkled with perfume or aftershave.

Taste
Talk about how we taste sweet, sour, bitter, salty things. Other tastes are really smells. We all like different things. Have a selection of different fruits to try. Talk about people from other cultures and how their tastes are different and their cooking smells are different from ours e.g. strong curries, stir fried food, pasta, pizzas, garlic. Cut out magazine pictures of different foods - nice and nasty!

Instructions for Photocopiable Activities - Week 6

Mathematics

Sew a 4

Photocopy the 4 shape onto card and cut round it. Punch holes with a hole punch. Use bright coloured wool for the children to sew with. Wind some tape over the end of the wool to make it easier to push through the holes. Stick the other wool end to the back of the card. When finished, staple the 4 onto some paper and let the children draw a picture of themselves and practice writing 4. Point to the words 'I am 4'. How old will they be next?

Language and Literacy

Put a baby kangaroo in the pouch

Let the children try to cut out mother Kangaroo and the pocket. Cut round the baby for the children. They can colour mother and practice writing K on the baby. Staple on the pocket pointing out the word 'Kangaroo'. The baby can jump in and out of the pocket.

Knowledge and Understanding of the World

Let the children cut out the figure and the tongue, but make a mouth slit for them with sharp scissors or a cutter. The children can draw in a face, colour the figure and the tongue. Help them to concertina up part of the tongue and fix with tape through the slit so that the tongue extends when pulled. The children can cut out the pictures and choose which ones they want to stick on the figure. Point to the words to encourage early reading skills.

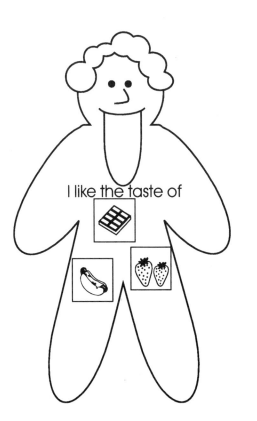

Mathematics - Week 6

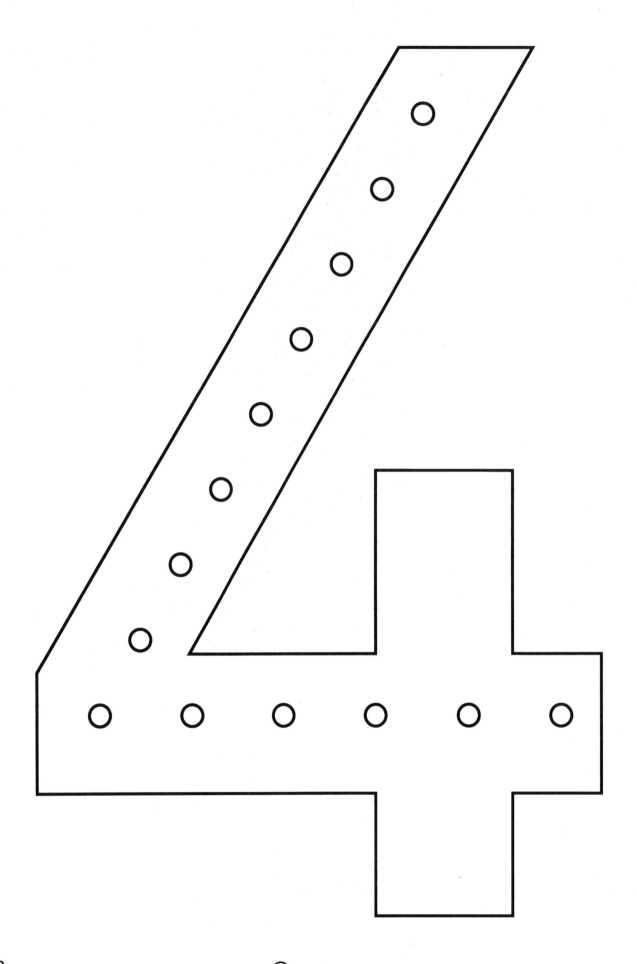

Language and Literacy - Week 6

K k
kangaroo

Knowledge and Understanding of the World - Week 6

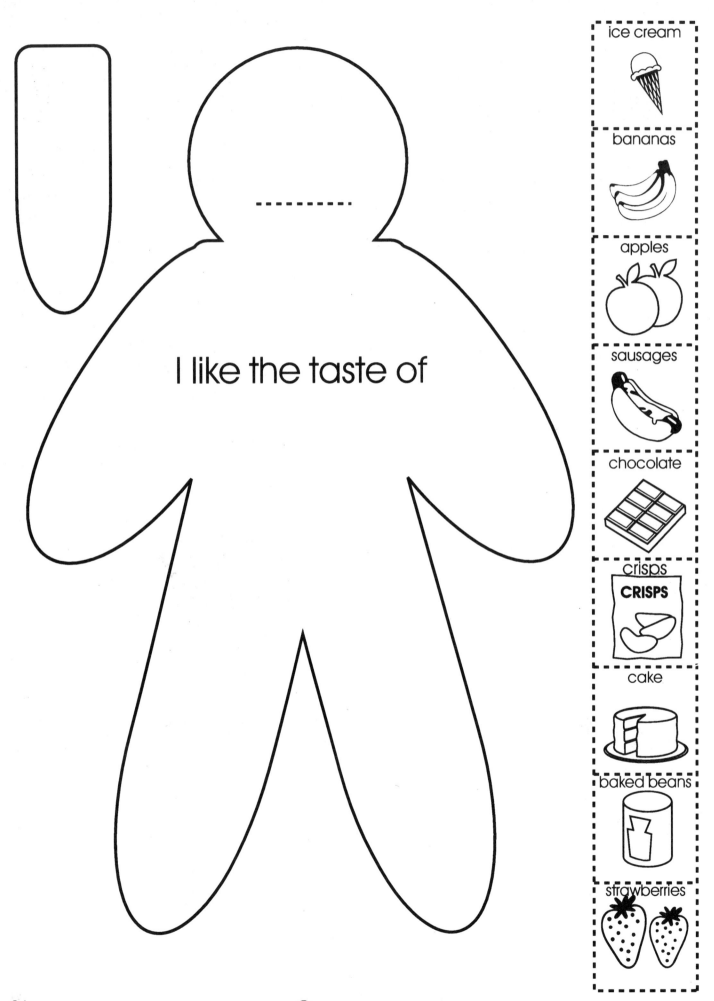

I like the taste of ....

ice cream
bananas
apples
sausages
chocolate
crisps
cake
baked beans
strawberries

Suggested Activities - Week 7

Mathematics - Recognising and Understanding Number 5 / Measuring

5 little sausages frying in a pan

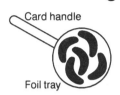

Sizzle, sizzle, sizzle, one went bang.

Cut out some sausage shapes and colour. Blu tak into pan. Remove to match rhyme.

Practice writing 5 on a five shape

I am going to be 5

Cut out some candles and stick on the cake using 2 colours of stickers on the candles.

Look at rulers and tape measures. Compare long and short paper strips, ribbons etc. Measure along tables, cupboards, bricks. Talk about shoe sizes.

Use strips of bright card or paper. Measure, cut and stick strips onto a triangle shape starting at the bottom. What happens to the strips - longest, shortest?

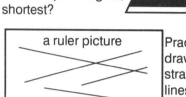

Practice drawing straight lines

Language and Literacy - Letter Mm Letter Nn

Mm Say 5 things about me

 I am a girl
I have short hair
I like cats etc.

or

Music

Listen to marching music

Make a mouse

Cut out a triangle shape.
Add ears, tail, whiskers. Practice m

Nn A night time picture

Talk about darkness, shadows, moon, stars, street lights, car lights, cats eyes, people who work at night, animals at night etc. Listen to night time sounds. Make a dark corner.

Cut out a moon shape. Print stars with fingertips.

I say no to

being unkind, pushing, being rude, snatching, grumping

Make a name necklace

Thread pasta beads, punched card.

Knowledge and Understanding of the World - Melting / Cold Countries

Talk about what happens when we melt things. What makes ice melt, snow, ice-cream etc? Make some chocolate cornflakes. Watch the margarine, chocolate, syrup and sugar melt.

Talk about what happens to wax crayons left in the sun, tar on the road on long hot days etc.

Look at pictures of countries where there is a lot of ice and snow. Talk about people who go ski-ing, contrast between winter and summer weather etc.

Talk about animals who live in cold countries - how they keep warm and hunt for food.

What happens when ice melts?

Story - Bother with Boris - *Dianna White - ABC Publications, All Children's Co*

Instructions for Photocopiable Activities - Week 7

Mathematics
Number 5 game
Cut out the number 5's and the game box for each child. Make a number 5 dice by using a cubed brick and sticking 5 on 4 sides, leaving 2 sides blank. Point out the numbers and the patterns. The children throw the dice and stick a number 5 in each spot with a quick dab of glue, unless the dice lands on a blank side. The children colour the 5's when the game has finished.

Language and Literacy
Make a munching monster
Let the children cut out the monster head and the m shapes if they can, and practice writing m on the front. They can decorate the back of the monster. Let them make a tail and neck from scraps of paper and stick them (or use split pins) onto the monster. They can join the head together with a split pin or pin the head to the neck. The children can practice saying Mmmm as the monster moves and munches.

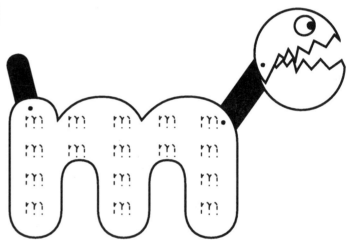

Knowledge and Understanding of the World
Melting candles
Let the children watch some different shaped candles melt and look at the hot wax. Talk about what happens when it cools. Let them colour the candles on the sheet that they think have melted. What signs on the candles will they look for - a flame, not just the wick, melted wax on the sides? Which candles have been burning the longest time?

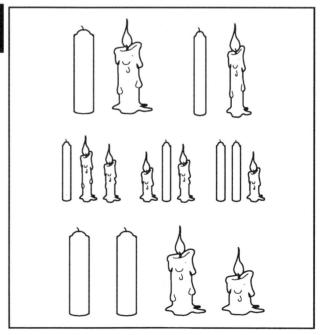

Mathematics - Week 7

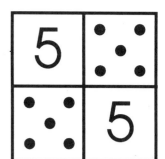

Language and Literacy - Week 7

Knowledge and Understanding of the World - Week 7

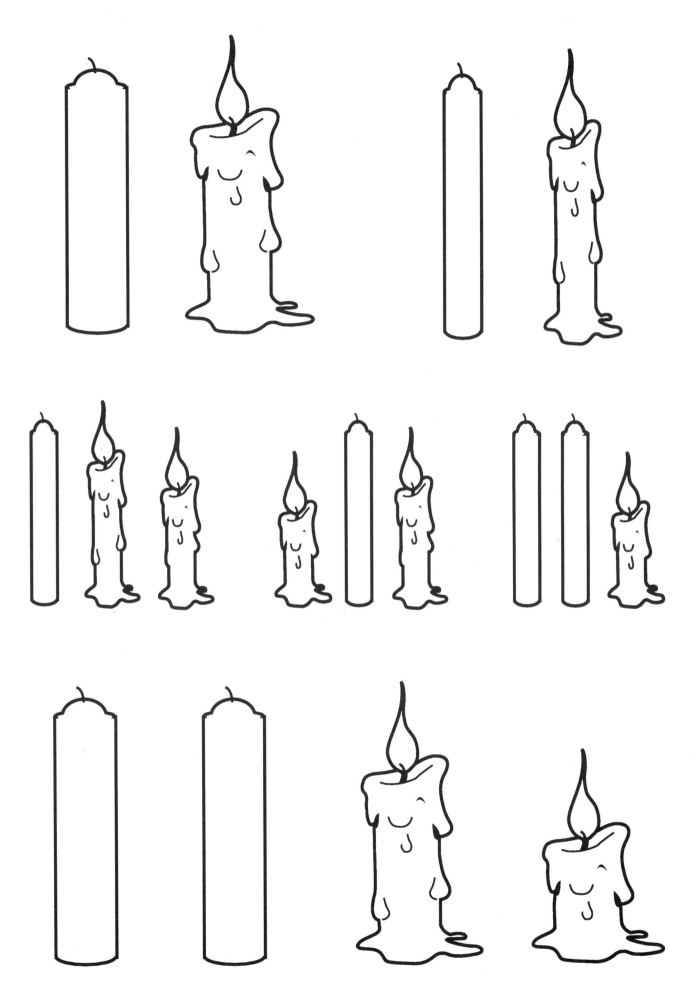

Suggested Activities - Week 8

Mathematics - Recognising and Understanding Number 6

Make a picture

Draw, cut, or stamp 6 pictures.

Threading strings of 6

Thread some pasta or collage bits onto some wool. Attach to some card. Write numbers 1-6 as the children count.

Sorting circles
Use paper plates with a big 6 written on. Let the children put objects on in two colours to make 6.

Make a family of 6
Cut out little people holding hands for the children from folded paper. Let the children colour and count them.

Language and Literacy - Letter Oo Letter Pp / Rhyming Words

Oo Make an Octopus
Staple 2 head shapes partially together and let the children stuff with torn newspaper. Finish stapling. The children stick on dangling legs and paint on a face. Hang up.

An orange tree
The children practice writing o on 'oranges' that they cut out. They draw a tree and stick the oranges on.

Rhyming words
Play games with words that rhyme - bee tree, pen hen, fish dish, shell bell, fox box, cat hat, mouse house, car star, pear bear etc.

Draw a cat
Let the children draw a cat. Give them words and rhyming pictures to stick on.

Pp A pig post box
Let the children cut out a pig face and stick on the end of a small box. Make a slit for them on top of the box. The children practice writing p on paper to post in the box. (Use a box that will open at the end to retrieve the p's).

Print a pretty pink parrot
Let the children use scrunched paper to print on a parrot shape with pink paint. Use pink crepe for a tail.

Knowledge and Understanding of the World - Floating and Sinking / Boats

Collect a variety of objects to experiment with eg:

coin, button, wooden spoon, nail, pencil, metal spoon, peg, sponge, wooden brick, cork, jay cloth, feather, oil and flour.

Talk about the objects and what they are made of. Let the children predict what will happen when they are dropped into water. Will it float, or sink quickly or slowly? A deep clear container of water is best for the children to see easily.

Look at pictures of different kinds of boat - a yacht, ocean liner, old sailing boat, rowing boats, punts, rafts used long ago, gondolas, canoes etc.

Let the children experiment making their own boat - give them some pieces of wood, corks, margarine tubs, lids, plasticine, paper, small sticks etc. Will their designs stay afloat on water?

Talk about where people sail boats - rivers, water ways, lakes, reservoirs, the sea. Look at the map or globe to see where the oceans of the world are.

Instructions for Photocopiable Activities - Week 8

Mathematics

Number 6 game

Cut out the 6 shape and make a number 6 dice using a small cubed brick and sticking 6 on 4 sides, leaving 2 blank. The children throw the dice and put a cube or counter on each pattern of 6 on the 6 shape unless the dice lands on a blank side. They can colour the spots and the 6 when the game has finished. (The game can become very slow if they colour the spots whilst playing).

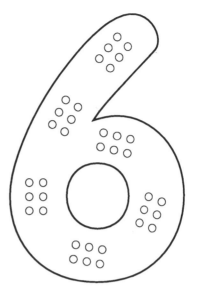

Language and Literacy

Rhyming words - a bee in a tree

Let the children colour and cut out the tree. Cut round the bee for them. Punch a small hole in the tree and let the children thread some wool through. Make a large knot for them at the back. The children can help to tape the wool on the back of the bee. By pulling the bee or the knot, the children can make the bee fly on and off the tree. Point to the rhyming words and help them to hear the rhyming sounds.

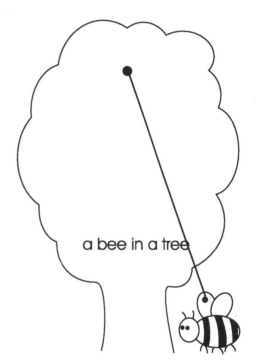

Knowledge and Understanding of the World

Floating and sinking

After discussion and experimenting with objects floating and sinking, let the children record their findings. Can they stick the pictures they have cut out in the tank where they feel it is appropriate?

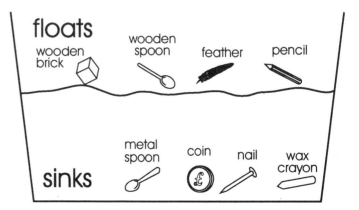

Mathematics - Week 8

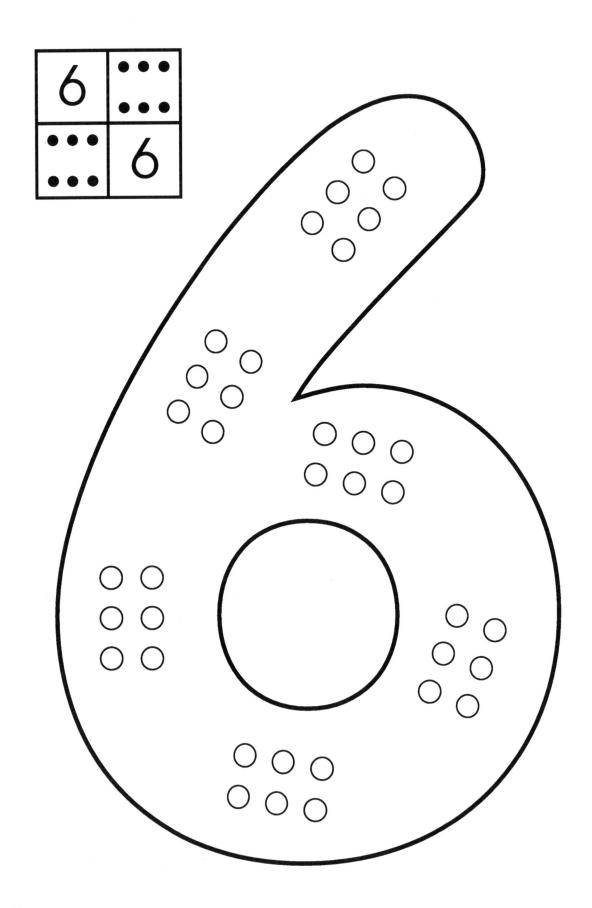

Language and Literacy - Week 8

a bee in a tree

Knowledge and Understanding of the World - Week 8

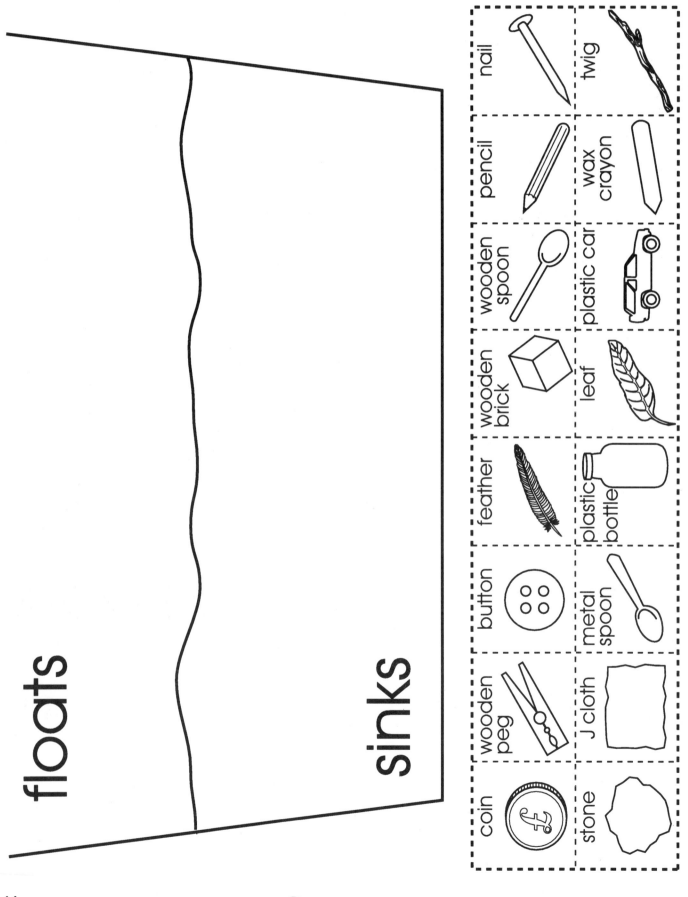

Suggested Activities - Week 9

Mathematics - Recognising and Understanding Number 7

Number 7 collage

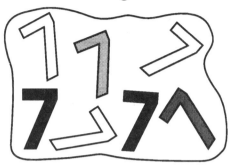

Give the children some cut out 7 shapes in a variety of sizes and from different types of paper e.g.- foil, material, wall paper etc. Let the children make their own design sticking the 7's onto paper.

Sorting and counting 7's
Cut out some large 7's to sort and count 7 of things on eg. - buttons, cars, cubes, animal shapes etc.

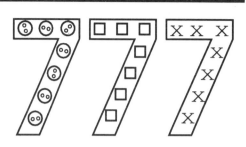

Play some games

1 Take 7 giant steps. Stretch up 7 times. Do 7 little jumps. Make a ring with 7 children.

2 "I went to the shop and bought".
7 apples (repeat),
7 apples, 7 bananas and....,
7 apples, 7 bananas, 7 tomatoes.

Language and Literacy - Letter Qq Letter Uu Letter Rr

Qq Things I can do

 Brush my hair
Clean my teeth
Clap my hands
Run down the path

 Tip toe
Say my name
Read a book
Breathe

Uu Things I can see up in the sky
- birds, sun, helicopters, aeroplanes, hot-air balloons, flags, stars, moon, bees, aerials etc.

Rr Make a red robot
Cut out a variety of red shapes for the children to design a robot. Let them practice writing **r**.

Rr Action words
running, racing, reaching, rowing, rolling, rambling, robbing, reading, returning.

Move like a Rusty Red Robot

Knowledge and Understanding of the World - Magnets

Give the children magnets to experiment with and a variety of objects to use e.g.-

Nails
scissors
button
paper clips

feather
teaspoon
keys

paper
little brick
bottle top

Ask the children to predict what they think will happen when the magnet touches the objects.

Sort into sets | attracts | | does not attract |

Look at a compass and talk about how it will always show where the direction North is, using a small magnet, which ever way it is turned.

Sailors in the past first used compasses to find their way when clouds covered the sun and stars that normally guided them.

People who go hill walking, mountaineering or sailing use compasses to help stop them getting lost.

Instructions for Photocopiable Activities - Week 9

Mathematics

Snow White and the 7 Dwarfs

Let the children cut round the house and fold in the sides. They can draw the windows and door on the front. Inside the children can draw Snow White, and then cut up in between the dwarfs and stick them in the centre part. Help them to look at the numbers on the dwarfs and practice counting.

Language and Literacy

Make a Queen with her umbrella

Let the children cut out the Queen's dress and decorate it with shiny coloured foil. They can colour the sash blue, and then stick the dress onto a larger piece of paper. They can then draw in the face, arms and legs. Let them cut out the crown and stick on pretend jewels to go on the Queen's head. They can colour and cut out the umbrella to stick next to the Queen and draw in the handle.
The children can practice writing q and u.

Knowledge and Understanding of the World

My magnet attracts

After experimenting with magnets and a variety of objects, the children can record their findings. Let the children cut round the magnet and in between the pictures of objects. With discussion, help them to decide which objects they want to stick on the magnet. Point out the words to them.

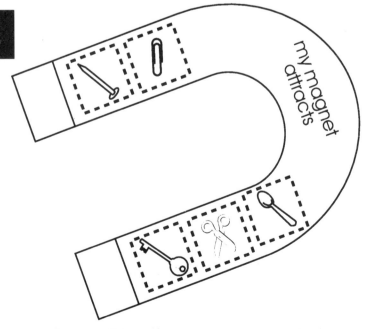

Mathematics - Week 9

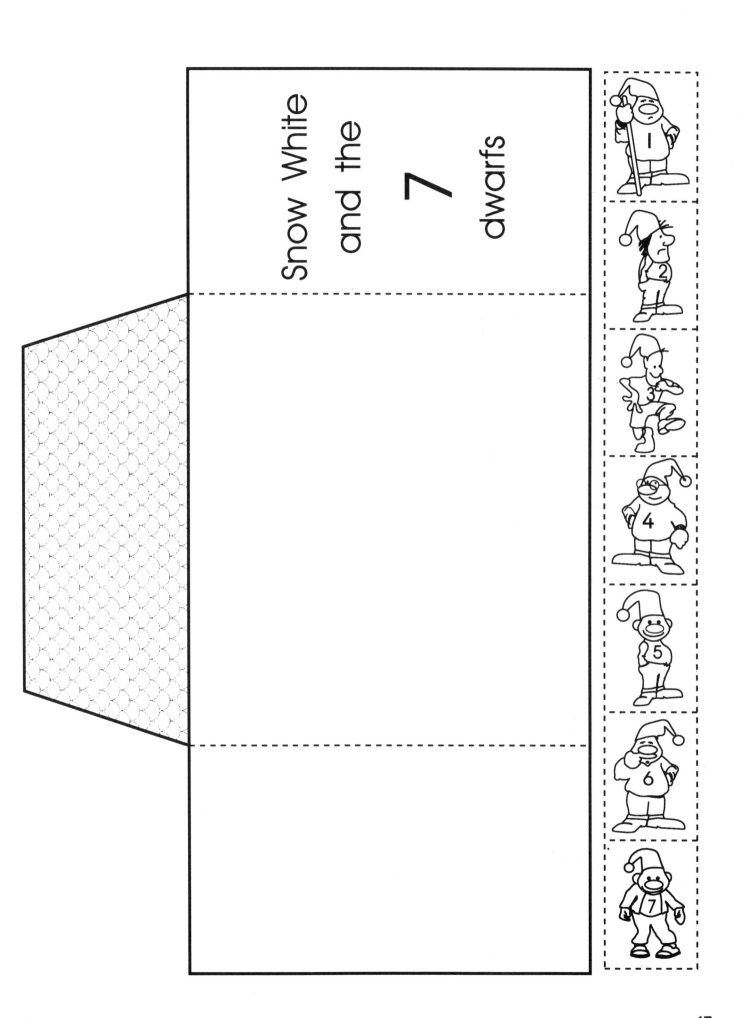

Language and Literacy - Week 9

Knowledge and Understanding of the World - Week 9

Suggested Activities - Week 10

Mathematics - Recognising and Understanding Number 8 / Positions

Finger paint 8's
Finger paint number 8's on a table top or board. Press a piece of paper over to take a print.

Make a pretend train track

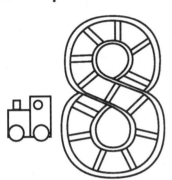

Cut out an 8 shape from card. Draw on lines to make a track. Make a pretend train with a small box and plastic top wheels.

Stick 8 legs on a spider
Cut out a circle of card and draw on a spider face. Colour or stick on sticky paper bits. Cut up strips of card for the legs and glue onto the back. Bend the legs and dangle.

Play games
taking 8 steps forward, backwards, to the right, to the left.

Incy Wincy Spider

Language and Literacy - Letter Ss Letter Tt

Ss Stick some snakes on an S

Cut out an S shape and an assortment of snakes - long, short, fat, thin. Colour and decorate the snakes and stick onto S shapes.

Make a picture of sea and sand

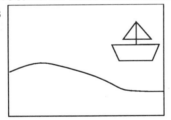

Make the sea using torn pieces of blue/green tissue. Paint the sand with yellow paint and glue mixed. Sprinkle on sand.

Tt Television
Talk about favourite programmes.

Telephones
Have some pretend conversations. Cut out telephone catalogue pictures.

Do actions to a tambourine

Have a teddies tea party
Send some invitations.

Rhyme - I'm a little teapot.
Draw some patterns on a teapot.

Knowledge and Understanding of the World - Soap / Water / Washing

Look at some different kinds of soap e.g.- powder, washing up liquid, soap flakes, bars of soap, liquid hand soap, bubble bath, shampoo.

Make bubbles with slippery soap. Talk about washing and which kind of soap would be used.
- washing clothes - in a machine or by hand
- washing dishes - in a machine or in the sink
- washing cars
- washing people.

Look at pictures of how people used to do washing in the past - old fashioned machines, mangles, wash tubs, coppers, wash boards etc.

Talk about how people in the third world countries do their washing if they have no machines or electricity - using rivers, carrying water on their heads from wells, pumps and rivers.

Instructions for Photocopiable Activities - Week 10

Mathematics
Where is the cat?

Talk about different positions as illustrated. Play games such as "Hunt the Thimble" emphasising positions. Let the children cut round the outside of the boxes and cut out the two trees. The cat may need to be cut out for them. The children can colour the two trees and stick them in the boxes as shown, leaving the tree trunk in the "behind" box without any glue on to lift up.

Let the children colour in the two walls and draw one person in the "beside" box, and two in the "between" box. Put some blu tak on the back of the cat, so that the children can move it about in the different positions saying where it is - ie. behind the tree, between the people etc.

Language and Literacy
Make a Tortoise

Let the children cut out the tortoise and colour it in. They could cut out some brown shapes from sticky paper or tissue to decorate the tortoise's back. Point out the word tortoise and the letter **t**.

The children can practice writing **t** on the other side.

Knowledge and Understanding of the World
Soap for washing me

Talk about all the different kinds of soap we use for washing ourselves. Experiment to see which makes the most bubbles, smells the nicest.

Look at the different consistencies. Let the children draw in the bubbles in the bath. Colour the bath and cut out and stick on the different types of soap. Point out the labels to encourage reading.

Mathematics - Week 10

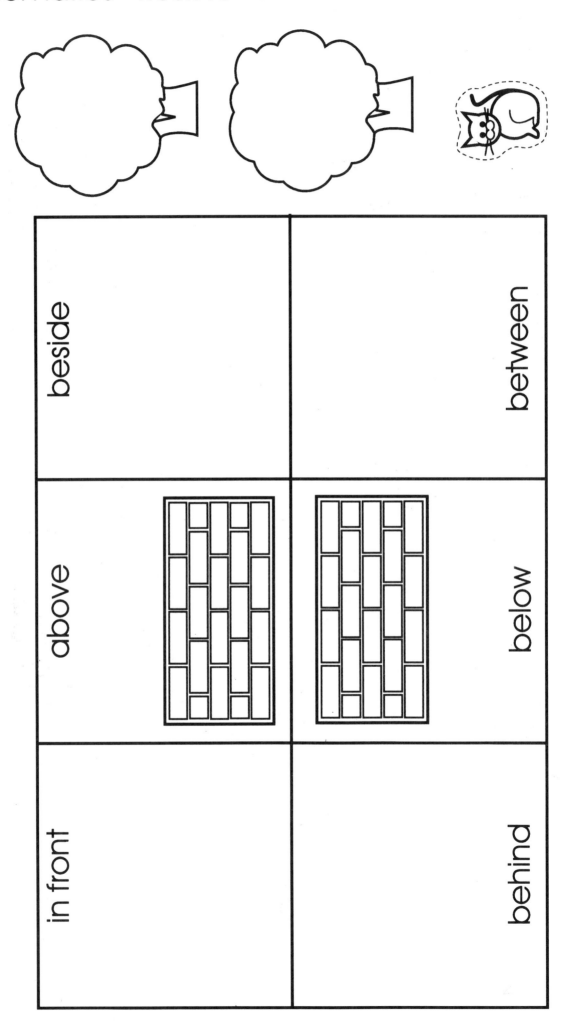

Language and Literacy - Week 10

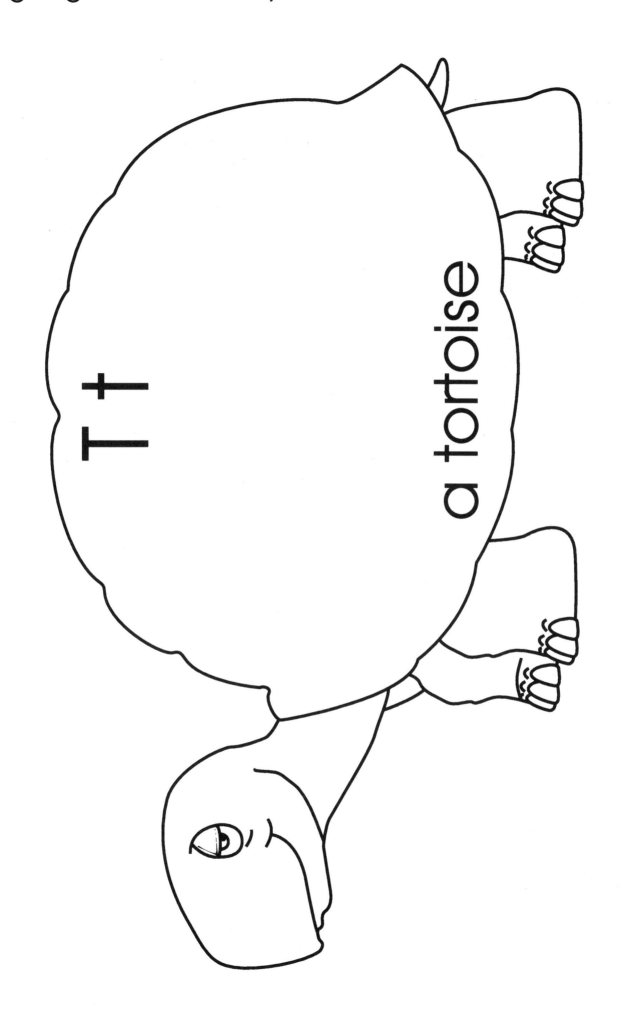

Knowledge and Understanding of the World - Week 10

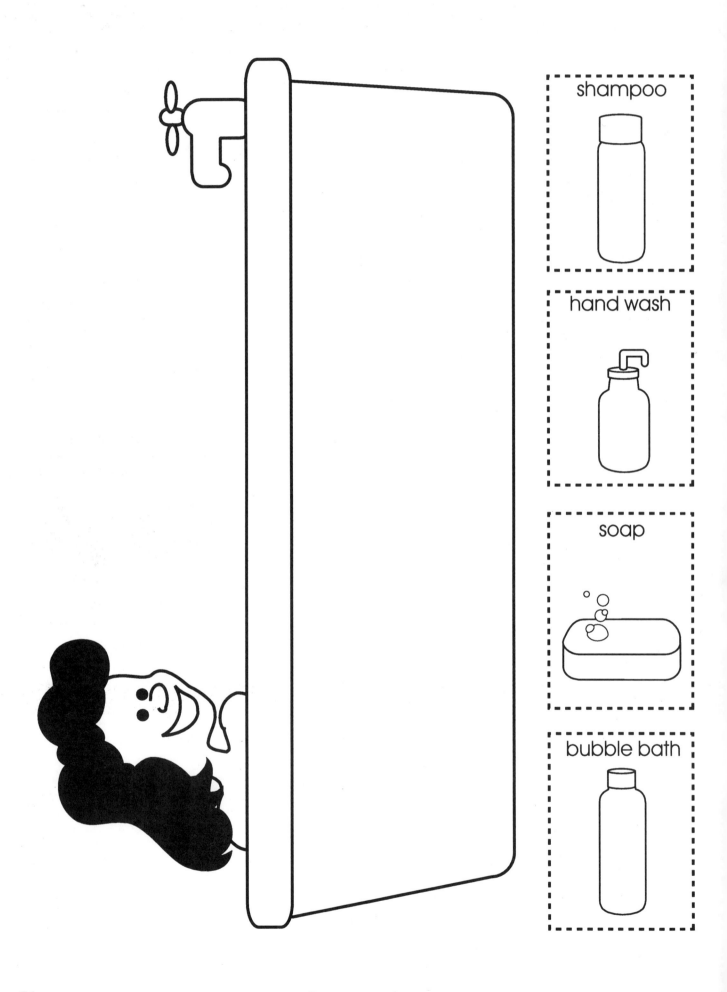

Suggested Activities - Week 11

Mathematics - Recognising and Understanding Number 9

9 fish in a bowl
Let the children cut round a bowl shape. Give them a variety of fish shapes and sizes to colour, count and stick in the bowl.

Dial 999
Make a mobile phone. Cover a small box with plain paper for the children to paint. Add a knob for an aerial and a card speaker at the side. Let them stick on the numbered spots.

Emergencies
Talk about dialling 999 - Fire, Police, Ambulance - being quick helping other people etc.

Make a "naughty" 9
Help children contrast 9 with 6. Let them cut out a 9 shape with a long tail. Cut and rejoin with a split pin to make the top part move. Make "naughty" 9 stand up straight not like 6

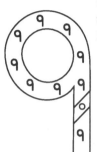

Telling the time clocks and watches
Talk about the different ways to tell the time e.g. - clocks, watches, sun dials. Make a collage from catalogue pictures of clocks and watches.

Song
My Grandfather's Clock

Make a paper plate clock with card hands fixed by a split pin.

Language and Literacy - Letter Vv Letter Ww

Vv Make a vase of violets
Use card to cut out a v shape on the fold for the children. Let them make violet tissue flowers and stalks to stick inside, that will show through the gap in the v.

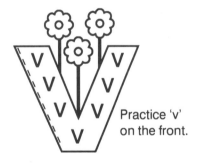

Practice 'v' on the front.

Vans
Let the children cut round a van shape and snip and stick little bits of coloured card or paper on to decorate it. What does it deliver?

Talk about favourite videos

Visitors
How do we behave? Are we welcoming, polite, friendly etc?

Ww A Whale in the waves
The children cut out a whale shape and colour it grey/black. Give them some wavy paper to stick onto a blue sea background with the whale at the back.

What is the weather today? - windy?

Knowledge and Understanding of the World - Growing Seeds

Growth
Help the children to :-

- plant cress on wet cotton wool in yoghurt tubs

- put a wet paper towel in a jar and put a bean between the towel and glass

- put a carrot top in water on a lid

- put a potato in the top of a jar with water in to see the roots grow.

Talk about conditions for growth - light, warmth, water, nourishment.

Point out the parts of a plant e.g.- seed, shoots, roots, stem, leaves, flowers.

Look at different seeds in packets. Cut out pictures from seed catalogues to make a collage. Do some gardening - digging, raking, planting, weeding. Talk about the tools you would use. Look at pictures of farmers in the past who sowed seeds by hand, and used horses to pull the plough. Look at old tools that were used.

Instructions for Photocopiable Activities - Week 11

Mathematics
Hickory Dickory Dock

Talk about times of day - morning, afternoon, evening, night, mealtimes and the things that we do such as - getting up, going to school, shopping, having a bath etc. Talk about the rhyme Hickory Dickory Dock - an old grandfather clock that chimes. Was the mouse frightened? When is it 1 o'clock?

Photocopy the activity sheet on card if possible.
Let the children colour the clock and mouse and cut them out. Make a slit for them on the dotted line with a cutter or sharp scissors. The children can fold over the base of the mouse, tuck in through the slit and slide the mouse up and down as they say the rhyme.

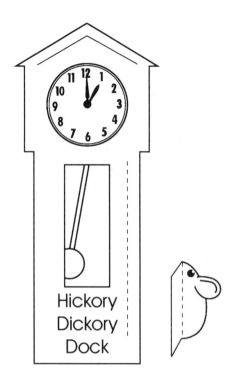

Language and Literacy
Make a wiggly worm

Have a look at some garden worms with the children and talk about how they help plants to grow by making holes that let air into the soil. Sing the song "Wiggly Woo" (This Little Puffin). Let the children cut out the "w" shape and the worm, colour them and practice writing w. Cut out the three holes for the children so that they can make the worm wiggle through them.

Knowledge and Understanding of the World
The story of a seed

Talk about making up a story - what happens at the beginning, middle, end. Having looked at seeds, grown some and talked about the different parts of a plant, let the children cut out the pictures on the dotted lines and colour them in. Ask what is happening in each picture and which one should be first. They can stick the pictures in order from left to right in the blank boxes, and then tell the story.

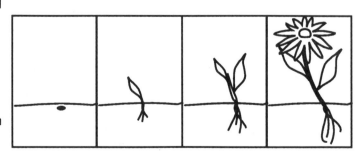

Mathematics - Week 11

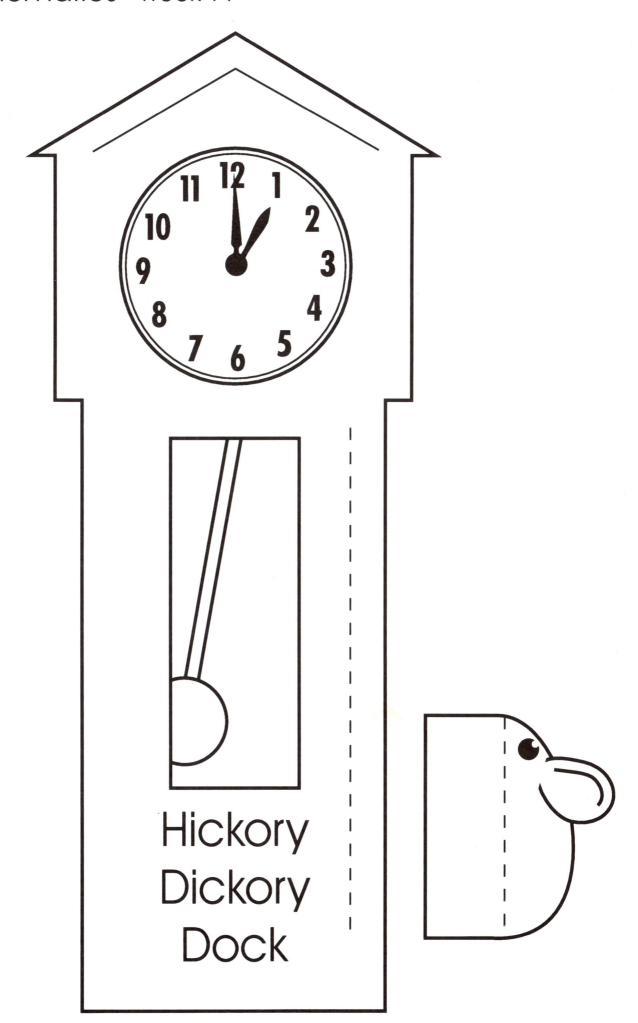

Language and Literacy - Week 11

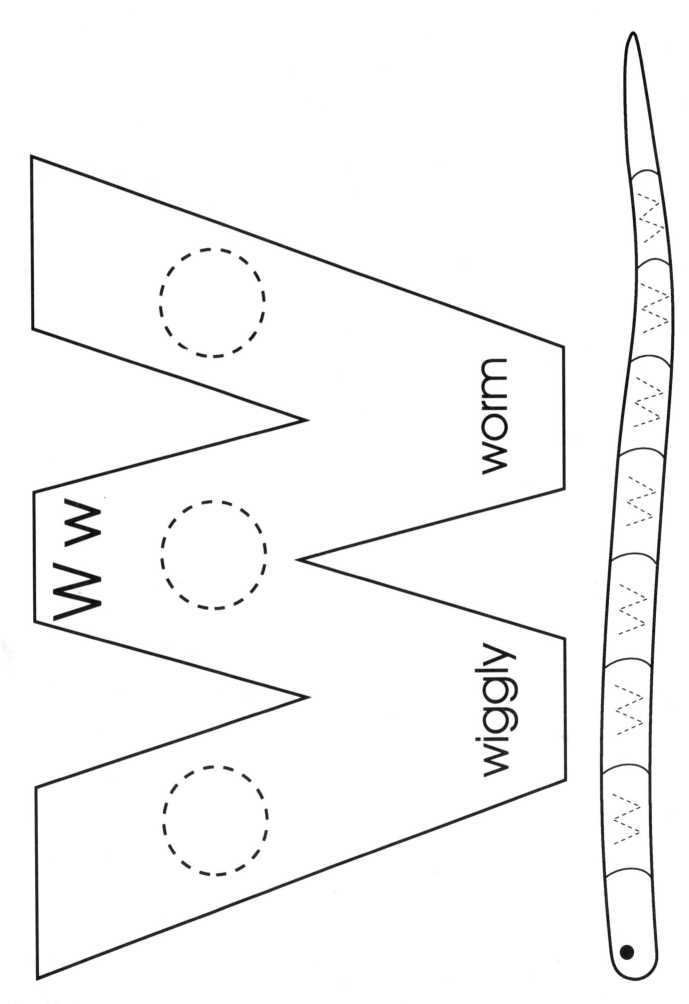

58

Knowledge and Understanding of the World - Week 11

The story of a seed

Suggested Activities - Week 12

Mathematics - Recognising and Understanding Number 10 / Money

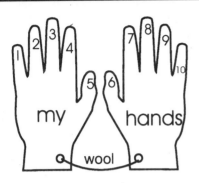

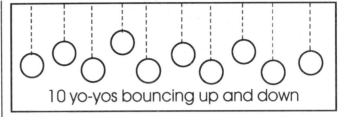

10 little fingers and thumbs
Help the children to draw round their hands and cut them out. Write in the numbers for them as they count, colour and join.

10 Yo-yos
Yo-yos bouncing up and down.
Let the children colour the yo-yos and draw in the strings. Count them all.

Rhymes
10 green bottles hanging on a wall.
There where 10 in a bed.

Make a 10 mobile
Cut out a flower shape with 10 petals for the children to paint, then stick a bright 10 on and thread 10 things to hang.

Language and Literacy - Letter Xx Letter Yy Letter Zz

Xx Talk about the words with x in
ie. fox, box, axe, ox, oxo.
Let the children make a letter for mummy and draw kisses.

Yy Have a go using a yo-yo

I say yes to
- ice-cream
- staying up late
- going to the beach

Make a yacht
Let the children cut out a yacht shape and stick on circles for portholes. Give them tissue paper and card to make their own flag.

Zz Count down from 10 to zero
Make a zig zag zoo book.
Let the children cut out pictures of zoo animals from cards, calenders or magazines to stick in a book.

Zips
Look at different sizes of zips.

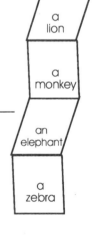

Knowledge and Understanding of the World - Camouflage

Camouflage
Look at some pictures of animals to see how their colour blends in with the place where they live to protect them from danger e.g.-

- Tiger stripes blend in with the light and shadows of the jungle

- Zebra stripes look like the light and shadows of the grass land areas.

Some animals change colour to fit in with their background such as frogs who become brown or green depending on where they are.

Octopus and chameleon change fairly rapidly. The arctic brown hare changes colour in winter to look white like the snow.

Look at stick insects and see how they look like twigs and leaves. Talk about where wild animals live and look at a globe or map to find the different countries.

Instructions for Photocopiable Activities - Week 12

Mathematics
Make a purse for money

Have a selection of coins for the children to look at, identify and sort. Find all the 10p coins. Talk about what we use money for and where we keep it e.g.- purses, wallets, piggy banks, pockets, banks etc.

Where do we get money from? - post offices, banks, cash points, cash back in shops.
Let the children make some rubbings of coins, by putting thin paper over a coin and crayoning over the top. Help them to cut out several coins. They can cut round the purse and cut up the slit in each top, slot together to make the purse open and close. The children can colour the purse and stick their coin rubbings inside.

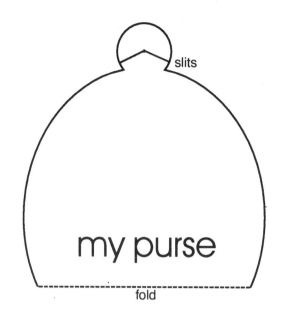

Language and Literacy
Colour some things yellow

y-yellow. Make a yellow display of different objects and shades.

Talk about things that are usually yellow such as bananas, corn-on-the-cob, chicks, daffodils etc.

Let the children colour in the pictures of yellow things.

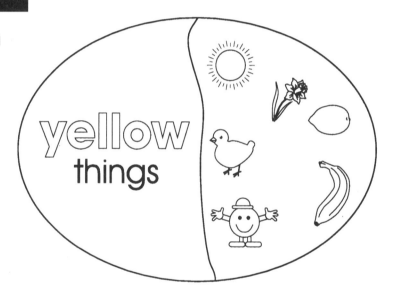

Knowledge and Understanding of the World

Let the children cut out the Zebra and draw some vertical black stripes on it.

Make a background scene by using white paper and making vertical line prints on it. The children can use the edge of a short strip of thick card dipped in black paint.

Either stick the Zebra straight onto the background, or make the Zebra stand out by sticking a thin box or wad of card behind it first.

Mathematics - Week 12

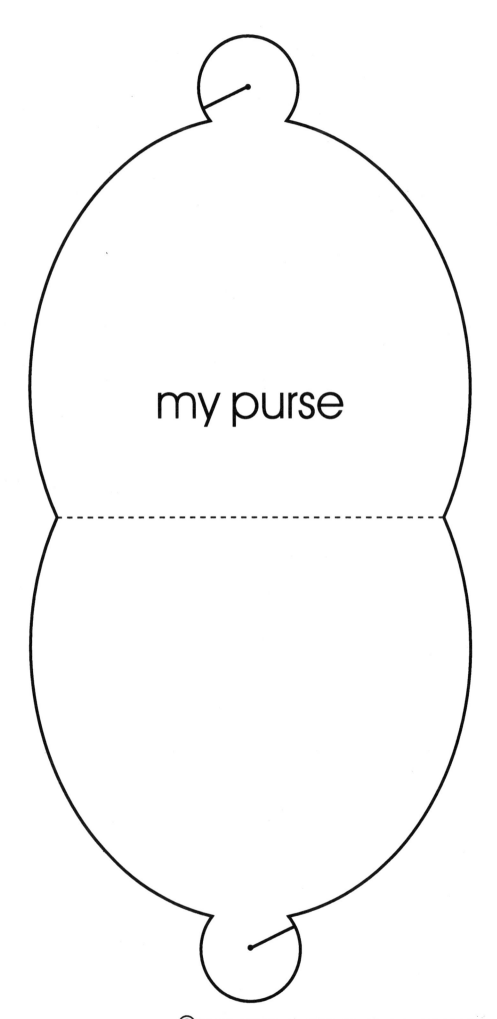

Language and Literacy - Week 12

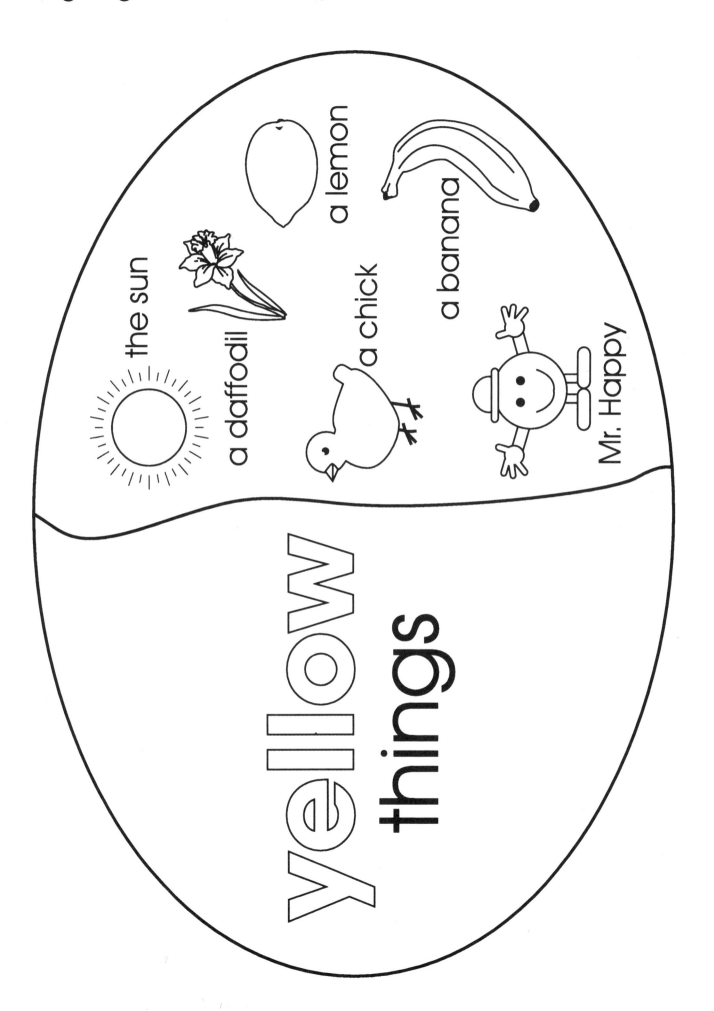

Knowledge and Understanding of the World - Week 12

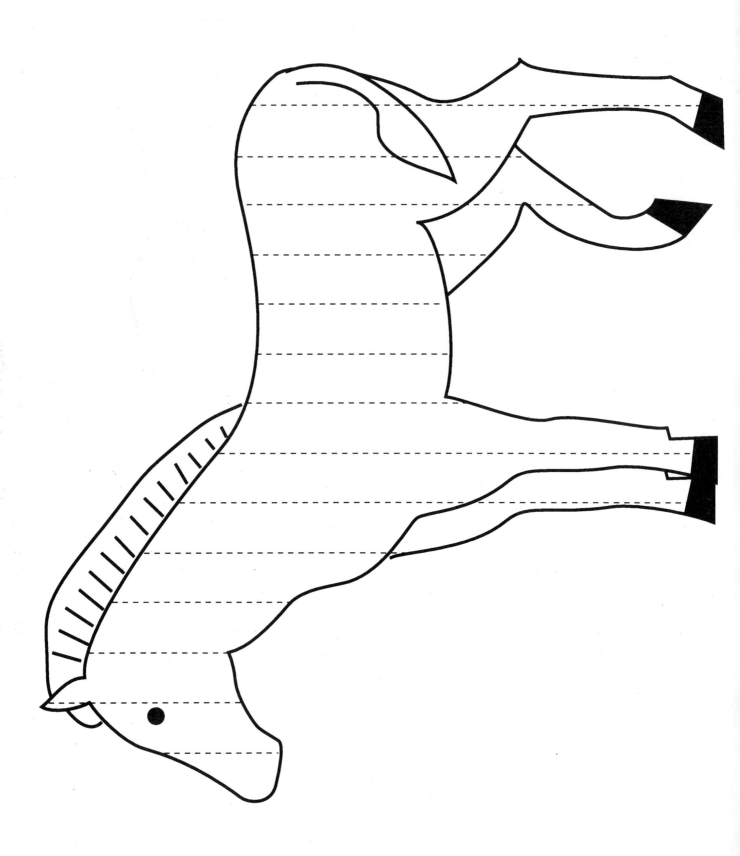